# Rum Humour

# Rum Humor

THADDEUS LOVECRAFT

Thaddeus Lovecraft

Published by Pillar International Publishing Ltd.

www.IndiePillar.com

Managing Editor: Sharon Moriarty

ISBN-13: 978-0-9574598-4-7

# DEDICATION

This is dedicated to Leonard, who laughed at my very first joke and with whom I continued a written correspondence over many years, across many cities, with increasingly disturbing subject matter.

Thaddeus Lovecraft

## ACKNOWLEDGMENTS

Special thanks to all of the Old Litopians who provided some of the inspiration and much of the succour.

# 1 MELISSOPHILE

The crunching gravel gave way to soft, noiseless grass as we, Mr Grindling and I, approached the arbour leading to the overgrown acre at the rear of Spite House.

"I ate cats," said Mr. Grindling.

"You ate cats?"

"Aye, I do."

"You *still* eat cats?"

"No, you soft southern bastid. I fookin ATE cats."

"Oh, you *hate* cats."

"Tha's right. Don' trust them bleeders."

Atop the sickly grey arbour, a white cat, evidently the source of Mr. Grindling's diversion, studied our passage. If the animal was a resident of this abandoned demesne it

1

would certainly be perturbed by the sight of two tall men, such as my colleague and I, stomping through its kingdom in our beekeeper suits and black boots.

"D'ya see that bastid? D'ya see 'im?" Mr Grindling waved his dormant stainless steel smoker.

"Mr. Grindling, if you will, we are not here to concern ourselves with creatures of a feline disposition."

Mr. Grindling grunted and passed under the arbour.

In no way did he live up to the charming, bucolic gentleman that my associates in London had described. He was coarse in language and in manners; he suffered, or I should say I suffered, from noxious emissions both oral and of the fundament; when he wasn't noisily masticating, he was busy expectorating - a thoroughly detestable sort.

My little sins often brought me into the company of rum types and brigands. Consequently, I had become adept at moderating my behaviour and expert at concealing disgust, in order that my very particular objectives might be realised.

This day's goal lay twenty paces south,

in a white, wooden construction. *Apis Mellifera* – the European honey bee. My first encounter with this genus would, I was sure, engender a singular folio in my black book of sexual experiments.

From the off, I was careful not to betray to Mr Grindling the nature of my expedition. Once, coincidentally in a case involving *Felis Catus,* I brought a man into my confidence and was rewarded with a blackmail of sodomy. That misadventure did add a new, unexpected page to my book but it was not one that I cared to revisit.

"Mr. Grindling," I said, "I will need you to smoke them and-"

His thick, calloused hand covered my mouth, my nostrils filled with the acrid scent of old tobacco. "Quiet. I could kill you now. Couldn't I?"

I nodded as best I could under his grip.

"But," he said, "I jus' wan my money, don' I."

I nodded, faster than before and pointed to where my wallet lay beneath the beekeeper suit.

He released me.

"I 'ope you don' feel I was bein' too

3

aggressive. I jus' got burned by some London folk—if you follow me…"

A gentleman's greatest asset is his composure. Mr. Grindling was not a gentleman but *I* certainly was.

"Mr Grindling, I can see you have been much abused by a lesser grade of man than I. Trust me. I ask that you take my honour as your guarantee. My pocketbook is beneath these layers and currently unavailable but, would that you had asked, I would have paid you in advance."

Mr. Grindling bowed his head. "Sir, I apologise. Has been a bad day fer me. My wife is sleepin' wi' the costermonger and my only son is up before the magistrate tomorrow. He buggered a –"

"Please, if you may, I understand you have struggles but I have a job to do."

It is often the case in my adventures that trepidation is supplanted by a very workmanlike desire to *get the job done*. My proximity to the hive and the emergent buzzing of the occupants brought a heat to my scrotum and instigated a redirection of the blood supply from sinless organs to that satanic ogre in my undergarments.

"Mr Grindling - smoke them."

*

Taking three subdued honey-bees and inserting them through the gap in my cotton trousers was undoubtedly the most exciting act I had committed that week. I guided them gingerly into place and waited, whistling to myself and nodding intermittently to Mr Grindling, who I had bade keep his distance, lest the insects infect him with the chronic disease which I had assured him was my *raison d'être ici.*

"Are they all right, sir?" Grindling called, edging closer to me.

I shook my fist. "Damn and blast your socks, man! Keep your distance. These things are lethal. Lethal, I tell you."

He edged back to the arbour. My attention returned to the awakenings in my undergarments: tiny tickles sent a wave of pleasure through me; the delicious anticipation building to what I hoped would be a crescendo like no other.

*

I believe what happened next is called anaphylaxis. But for Mr. Grindling and his tincture of epinephrine I would not be here today. In a quiet ceremony, later that week, I married him and although many would say it was biologically improbable, he is now pregnant with our fourth child.

## 2 SOME DRINK TO FORGET. SOME FORGET TO DRINK.

"Now officers, where was I? Oh yes... Let me tell you the story."

*

The tall, thin one pointed to the short, fat one. "I'm not the angry kind. But Mickey 'ere, he's got a fing 'bout people what breaks promises."

Mickey moved his baseball bat from one shoulder to the other, winking and twitching.

"His mum never loved him none: left 'im in the canal, she did," said the thin one.

"You know, young man," I said, rubbing at some ink on my hand that just would not come off, "I'm only a poor old lady

7

doin' her best to scratch together a few dimes to keep my Cecil here in lextrickery for his here wheelchair." I smiled and gestured at my beloved and, on cue, a fat gob of dribble bubbled from his mouth and ran right down his chin on to his precious Navy uniform. Now, he was so proud of that uniform and kept it so clean and buttons all polished, I hated to see him dirty himself: it's not what he would've wanted. So I took my rag and I wiped his chin and scrubbed at that lapel.

"Lady, lady," a voice came from behind me.

"Now boys, what can I do for you? Would y'all like a cold beer?"

The thin one had very narrow eyes. "We's 'ere for the money. 'Arry's money!"

"Harry? Who's Harry? Is he that nice man from Wyoming, always has a Michelob and roasted nuts...has the problems *down below*?" I whispered the last bit because that's how I was brought up. "Does he need money for his operation?"

The fat one, Mickey, he went all a-twitch. And, if I'm not mistaken, I'd swear he was ready to swing that bat if the thin one hadn't stepped in.

"Lady," the thin one said (I think, from

his accent, he might've been British), "'Arry Boscombe paid you a visit last week, lookin' for some money what you owed 'im for services delivered, like, an' you said you'd pay 'im today on account of the fact that your pension pays out today."

"You'll have to speak up, young man, your accent's kinda funny."

"LADY, WE'RE 'ERE FOR 'ARRY'S M–"

"Wait, I've just remembered something. My pension's paid today."

"That's what I've been sayin'. So 'ave you got the money for 'Arry?"

"Harry?" I said. "Who's Harry?"

The thin one turned to the fat one, Mickey I think he was called, and I'm pretty sure he used that 'F' word.

"Lady, this is your last chance. Eight hundred notes or Mickey 'ere will send your husband on an 'ome run."

Mickey stood over Cecil and, I'll declare, he made a swinging gesture that, if completed, would have knocked poor Cecil's head clean off.

"Now boys, please. Your mommas didn't raise you to be so unkind."

The fat one, Mickey I think was his

name, made a grunting noise and twitched something awful. He pulled back his bat and he was so mean looking I thought he just might do it.

"Okay. Okay. I'll get you your money. But you tell your Harry that I want a receipt for the IRS."

The thin one, Mickey I think he was called, snickered.

Next thing I know, I'm in my kitchen with eight-hundred dollars in my hands. And I don't know why I'm there and I look on my wrist where I've written 'gun' in black ink. So I get out my shotgun.

*Next* thing I know, I'm back in the bar and I'm hollering "Vincent, Vincent, come quickly. I've done a bad thing." And those two nice boys are lying there, *both* of them twitching, leaking blood all over my nice floor.

God bless my Vincent, the only one of my sons that lived: strong as an ox but none too smart. He's such a help.

"Ma, where will I put these ones?"

"*These* ones? Why, you say that like there are others. God made you soft, my strong boy. Not enough oxygen, the doctors said." And I went away chuckling to myself, rubbing at that word on my wrist. You know, it never did come out.

*

Now, can I get you two nice police officers a cold beer? Or a sandwich? How about I go into the kitchen and fix you up a nice sandwich...?

BANG. BANG.

"Vincent, Vincent. Come quickly. I've done a bad thing."

# 3 TWISTED

Sarah fingered the crumpled scrap of paper. Her sister had shoved it into her handbag and winked. She had been crying then. She was crying now. The apartment was mourning the loss of the LCD television, the Charlie Chaplin statuette, half the DVDs and all of the best books. She bit her lip and snuffled into her hot chocolate. *How could he?* Out the window of her apartment, sheltered from the bleak winter rain, she guessed that Roger was with *her*. He probably wasn't dressed in a duvet. He probably hadn't missed a week of work. He was probably sipping champagne.

"Can we start over?" he'd said, as she set fire to a pair of his boxer shorts.

"I still love you, honey. I'm sorry," he'd

said, as she cut the lipsticked collar off his pink shirt.

"You're making too much of this. It was just one time," he'd lied as she threw his damning mobile phone out the window.

She laid out the piece of paper and pressed it straight, leaning on the crumples with the heel of her hand. Her nails were shocking. She didn't want to think about how her face looked. Reading the note, she giggled. Her sister never liked Roger. She always said that his hair was too well kept for monogamy, his shoe collection too large for commitment.

The address on the page, a pub about twenty minutes on the other side of town, winked at her. She was going to go. One glass of Merlot, for luck.

*

"Can we start over?" said Frank, wiping up the wine with the sleeve of his jumper. "I'm not very good at these things."

They noticed it at the same time - a splash of Merlot on her white blouse, on her left breast to be more precise. Sarah sat open-mouthed as he grabbed her napkin and dabbed the stain, her arms unsure whether to push him away or to smack him. Was he copping a feel?

He stopped mid-stroke. "Oh my God, what am I doing?"

"What *are* you doing?"
He blushed. "The stain...I was...the stain."

"You can probably take your hand off my breast now."

"Yes, yes, of course." He sat down and adjusted the knot of his tie, twice.

What was he doing wearing a tie and a jumper to speed dating? Did his mother dress him?

"Did your mother dress you?"
He blushed.

"Don't answer that. Why am I such a fruitcake? That was a stupid thing to say."

Sarah sat in the nervous silence, regarding the dark wine blotch on the sleeve of his beige jumper; the way his hair seemed to be flattened, against its own will; the way his big coarse hands fidgeted; the way his blue eyes regarded her...

"You have sad eyes," she said.

"Is that a good thing or a bad thing?"

"It's just a thing. Not good. Not bad. Okay. Let's do this. Let's start over." She reached to shake his hand. "I'm Sarah, I'm thirty-five and I like good wine, preferably in a glass, and I like Mahler and Degas. I'm an accountant but don't tell anyone."

At the moment of connection, as his skin touched hers, a tiny line of static electricity jumped between them. *Chemistry,* thought Sarah.

"I'm Frank, I'm thirty-six and I'm a plumber. Sorry about the hand- shock thing. It's these bloody shoes. Rubber soles."

"A plumber?"

"Is that a good thing or a bad thing?"

"A good thing."

He smiled. What nice teeth. Roger had nice teeth. Roger had secrets.

"Do you have any secrets? Any children, a wife maybe?"

"I've two kids, yeah."

She stood up and pointed at him. "Aha!"

"My wife passed away two years ago."

She sat down, the weight of a roomful of stares bearing down on her. "Oh, I feel like a right shit now. Sorry, it's just that my ex, Roger the bastard, had – Oh, your eyes. That's the sadness. Do you miss her?"

"Every day."

"Aw love, why are you here? You can't

be ready for all this."

"I miss her. I miss a warm hug, a shared laugh, a kiss. I miss a whole lotta things. I kinda asked her in my head last night if I could move on and, in my head, she said *yes*. Does that make any sense?"

A snuffle escaped. "I miss that too." A single tear trickled down her cheek. He moved to brush it away but stopped. She took his hand and held it in hers. "I'm all weepy, now."

His eyes had a pre-tear glisten. "Don't start, or I'll start."

They both snuffled.

A thin-lipped woman in a fluorescent-pink Lycra top, all breasts and blonde hair, leant into their space. "It's my go now. Didn't you hear the bell?"

Sarah let go of his hand and wiped her eye. "Oh, the bell. Yes, of course." She looked around and yes, everybody was moving tables and clattering chairs. "Well, I guess it's goodbye then." She stood up. At the next table there was a young man in his early twenties. He had a snake tattoo on his arm and something, maybe an 'E', shaved into his crew-cut. She sat down again.

"I think I'll stay here if you don't

mind. Do you mind, Frank?"

"No...no, not at all." There were those teeth again and maybe, just maybe, the beginning of a sparkle in those blue eyes.

The thin-lipper, Kylie by her name-badge, folded her arms. "It's the rules, love. You have to move on."

Sarah took a second to reflect. Nice Frank or possibly homicidal tattoo bloke? "Kylie, can you just wait two seconds while I sort this out."

Kylie rolled her eyes. "Whatever."

Sarah leaned over to the next table. She read the crew-cut's name badge. "Troy, I'd like you to meet Kylie, I think you two kids will really hit it off. You do like breasts, don't you Troy? Would you mind swapping with Frank here?"

Troy smirked, winked at Kylie and swapped seats.

*

"And then, Roger, the bastard, told me that the knickers were his!" Sarah snorted with laughter.

Frank looked at his watch. "Oh God."

"What? Did I say something wrong? Was it the snorting?"

"No, no—the snorting is you. It's

funny. You're funny." Frank pointed at his watch. "The babysitter. I have to go."

"Yes, yes, of course. Go. Go. You go."

"I've really enjoyed myself. Thanks."

A couple pushed past Frank and he stumbled forward, his body now within a breath of intimate. He smelt of vanilla. Sarah sensed a kiss coming. Something brief and anxious that would have a hint of teenage about it. She was ready if he was. She willed her eyes to be caring and alluring with just a scintilla of lust.

"You should probably ask me for my number, then." *Why didn't he just go ahead and do it?* Sarah wondered if her eyes were saying more about the four glasses of Merlot than the beat of her heart. His eyes were sparkling.

He checked his watch again and the spell was broken.

"Here – that's my business card. My number's there. I have to go." He opened the door of the bar and the rain pelted in. She'd forgotten that it was raining. The door swung closed and he was gone. Was that it? Sarah read the card twice, lingering over the number and address.

"Looks like you two hit it off."

"Sorry?"

It was the girl, Kylie. She had her arm around Troy and she was grinning like a Cheshire cat.

Sarah looked at the door. "Yes, I think we did. Look, do you mind, I have to go."

She burst into the cold, wet night, hoping that she might get one last glimpse of Frank. How silly. How girlish. How exciting. But there was nobody else on the footpath and, try as she might, the drivers in the night-time traffic were just shadows in the blur of rain and the blinding of car lights.

A van drove past the kerb, window down, horn beeping.

"Get in out of the rain you mad woman!" It was Frank.

"Where's my goodnight kiss?" Sarah called out. He couldn't have heard her.

She looked down at the card in her hand. *Frank Strong, Independent Plumbing Contractors.*

As she skipped down the street, in what she later would realise was entirely the wrong direction, she tried the name out for size - 'Sarah Strong. Mrs. Sarah Strong. Delighted to meet you – I'm Mrs Sarah Strong.'

*

Frank drummed his fingers on the steering wheel. His mother would be waiting when he got home. She would say "Well?" in that way she did, with her hopeful smile. He would say "Not this time, Mum. Looks like it's still just you, me and the girls."

There was one ghastly woman, though. He couldn't shake her all night. She seemed to be half-cut before the first bell rang. She knocked over a glass of Merlot and left it for him to clear up. Then, when he tried to rescue what looked like an expensive blouse from a fatal wine stain, she all but accused him of groping her. As if that wasn't enough, even after she found out he was widowed she talked incessantly about herself and her ex-boyfriend.

Frank turned into the long gravel drive and his headlights lit up the rows of oak trees that lined the way.

"Roger, you're well shot of that one, mate."

His old business card came in handy. She could be the stalking type. Definitely, probably. The way she stood in the rain outside the bar: soaked, looking every bit the drunken bunny-boiler.

Frank hoped that she got the message when he called her a 'mad woman.'

Emily and Sarah would be asleep by now, snuggled up with their teddy bears. He'd tip-toe into their room and breath in their beauty for a few minutes. There's a woman out there somewhere who will tuck them in and play mother-daughter games—*not tonight girls, not tonight.*

# 4 THE SLIMMER'S GUIDE TO CANNIBALISM

The pebbles in Mobius' pocket were chattering away about the decline in design standards in modern architecture. The hall, built just last year, was without adventure—whitewashed breeze blocks, uniform square windows and a floor that had those carpet tiles which might have been fashioned from hairy coconuts. Mobius looked from chair to chair, taking in the excess and corpulence of the meeting's attendees.

"Kill them all," said the pebbles. "Skin 'em alive."

"Sh!" he said.

"Pardon me?" said the woman in the

next chair in the circle of shame.

"I'm sorry," he replied. "I was talking to the...I was talking to myself."

He noticed that she had a smidge of cream, on the tip of her nose and was momentarily hauled out of his awkward predicament by this distraction. She also had a smear of chocolate on her chin. Mobius thought 'éclair'. Cream aside, she was a touch overweight (she wouldn't be here if she wasn't) but there was something remarkably beautiful, something coded in her genes that Mobius couldn't quiet describe but which caused a little involuntary jiggle in his tummy. Maybe it was her eyes.

"You're very brave," she said.

"Am I?"

"You are, you know," said the pebbles.

"You are," she replied. "Can't be easy being the only man in the group."

He leaned over to speak and her perfume, a vanilla scent, gave the jiggle a little more to work with.

"You've got a smidge on your nose - just there."

She blushed and turned away,

digging into her handbag.

"You've screwed that up," said the pebbles.

She was face down in her handbag with a mirror and a tissue but her discretion was drawing everyone's attention. Mobius knew the glances, the hidden smirks and the stifled snorts. Dieters can be so cruel.

"Don't mind them," he whispered. "They're just jealous of your good looks."

"Score," said the pebbles.

What had he said? Where in the name of Jehovah did that come from? His shirt collar began to feel very tight. She put the mirror and the tissue back in her bag and leaning over to him she whispered "Do you fancy a cake and coffee? I'm not really up to Weightminders this week."

He nodded and they left, to the confusion of their starving neighbours. His hand brushed hers on the walk to the door. Zing. They had connected.

*

Mobius counted the points associated with each butter-cream and chocolate delight. "I'm thinking that even looking at these cakes probably counts as one point."

She already had an éclair and a slice of walnut coffee cake on her tray. "Fuck 'em," she said, at once putting her hand to her mouth. "Oh, I'm sorry. That sounded so coarse."

He picked up a slice of pecan pie with toffee cream and a baked Alaska. "You're right - fuck 'em."

She laughed. It *was* her eyes.

"It's her eyes, definitely," said the pebbles.

*

The walk from the hall to Purdy's Pantry, a mere hundred yards, had been most peculiar. She didn't speak. She must have noticed the current of electricity when their hands had touched but she didn't say anything. He floated. It was like a superconductor of lurve pulled him frictionlessly by her side. Then, when they reached the shop door, she stopped and he almost bounced off her. She kissed him. No ceremony, no lead-up or dilly-dally – just direct lip to lip and slip of the tongue contact.

"I was just checking," she had said.

He didn't reply, except with his smile.

"Just making sure that there wasn't a misunderstanding. It's not about the cake, not really,"

The pebbles were stunned.

"I don't even know your name," he said to her, as he handed his credit card to the slim shopgirl.

She pushed out her breasts and pointed. It took a few blushing, embarrassing moments before Mobius realised that she was wearing a name badge.

"Sarah – I like that name."

"Nice breasts," said the pebbles.

"I'm –"

"You're Moby. Duh. You have a name badge too."

The way she said 'duh'—an insult between strangers or enemies—foreplay between lovers.

\*

"Exercise is half the battle," she said, sweat dripping from her sticky hair. "Let's go again."

Mobius managed to squeeze his oiled frame out from underneath her, rolling off the sweat-stained beige sheets on to the wooden floor. He panted and stood. "Dear Lord. Can I have a sandwich first, to build my energy? That was one hell of a naked rodeo."

"Why not? Make me one too, Tonto." She winked and slapped him hard on the arse.

"Except this time, can *I* be the man?"

"We'll see," she replied, winking. "We'll see."

Mobius walked like a cowboy from his studio bedroom into his compact kitchen, musing all the while about the new word he had learnt that evening: 'strap-on'. Now that was unexpected. Imagine that! An unusual surprise. The pebbles had remained uncharacteristically quiet throughout the ... the...*experience.*

The fridge door let out an unsatisfying groan as it swung open. The reason for this, doubtless, was the state of its contents. A lump of milk sat at the bottom of a bottle inside the door; a blue-green cheddar glowered on the top shelf; an avocado on the middle shelf had been reduced to a stain; and a single wilted lettuce leaf pined for merciful death on the bottom shelf. Mobius' stomach did a drumroll-rumble.

"Kill her and eat her," shouted the pebbles, from the trousers on the bedroom floor.

Mobius' glance moved from the wilted lettuce leaf in the fridge to the glinting Sabatier cleaver on the counter and back again, and back again, and back again.

"Well, if I must," he replied, closing the fridge door.

# 5 LANCE BOYLE & THE DISCOMBOBULATOR

### *The Discombobulator*
*'Only to be used for evil deeds. Not to fall into the hands of a good person.*

*Invented by Evilyn Badwick, the Discombobulator is used to confuse and torture teachers. On top of the black box you will see three buttons: a red one, a green one and a yellow one.*

*Press the:*

*Red button to make the teacher forget to give homework.*

*Green button to make the teacher ring the bell for home-time.*

*Yellow button to make the teacher melt.'*

\*

The instructions seemed straightforward. In

29

the pictures, part A slotted into part B using screws E1, B2 and C3. Easy. Then, according to the text, the main thronker is flagellated to the splonkforcer using the grip-trestle.

"What's a grip-trestle?" said Lance, turning over the pages of the booklet in vain. He held what he imagined was a thronker, though he couldn't be sure that it was the *main* thronker—they all looked alike. On the table was what he assumed to be a splonk forcer.

He jabbed uneasily at the mess of wires and melted plastic with his red screwdriver.

Fizzzzzzzzzzzzzz - BANG!

He jumped, knocking a shelf of black paint tins off the wall. The Discombobulator sparked and whined under a plume of grey smoke.

"Curses, ratfinks and budgies! I'll never be an evil genius!"

Fetid Boyle, father to Lance, popped his head into the lab, shaving foam covering his goatee'd chin.

"Everything okay?"

"Dad! I can't seem to make anything work. I'll never be proper evil."

"Don't you worry, my little death-ray,

you just have to work at it."

"But I do Dad! I work ever so hard b-b-but..." He began to cry.

"Now son, evil geniuses don't cry. How would it have looked if I started blubbing when I stubbed my toe robbing the old folks' home? Or when that wheelchair bloke gave me a dead-arm, do you think I cried?"

Lance sniffled, rubbing the snot from his nose with his black cape. "No, Dad."

"I'm off to steal milk from the orphanage. Clean up and I'll let you stay up to watch the Murder channel."

A smile broke across Lance Boyle's face.

"Put that smile away."

"Yes, Dad."

The door slammed. Lance took a deep breath, which became a long, shoulder-drooping sigh. The Lab was a wreck. Smoke stained the ceiling and blackened the table. Sparks from the dying apparatus had ignited the hay in Hammy's cage and the little fellow was slowly cooking in his spinning wheel. One of the paint tins had opened, spilling a river of darkness; another had smashed a hole in the floor. A hole in the floor?

Lance prodded the hole with the

proddy end of his broom. It was definitely hole-shaped. No animal, robotic or insect noises emanated from within, regardless of how fiercely he waggled the broom. He'd found holes before. Been bitten, electrocuted, taken prisoner by a giant ant overlord—you don't let these things happen to you twice.

A hole, an ordinary hole. No need to inspect closer. No need to reach down and have a feel around – absolutely no need whatsoever. But, what if there were poisons down there? Poisons that could be used to paralyze pensioners. Or a sacred stone? One that causes bishops to spoil their undergarments! No sense in *not* looking.

The hole was the length of Lance's arm and about the same in width. His nails scraped the bottom and sides, before his hands came to rest on something papery. It was, in fact, some paper, tied up with a black ribbon.

Doubtless, thought Lance, ancient instructions on how to summon earthquakes and make it rain pee. He chuckled. A cough of dust escaped from the pages as the ribbon slid off. The ink was faint but he could make out a few words on the first sheet. These were instructions.

Lance turned the page and inhaled sharply as an image came into sight. Unfamiliar, it wasn't. Shocking, it most certainly was.

\*

Fetid Boyle prised the tiny severed hand from the bottle, remarking to himself how persistent and dogged the little tykes were. The last bottle in place, he closed the fridge door.

Fetid jumped in alarm. "Janey Mackers and his seven bicycles!"

Lance had stood motionless, noiseless behind the fridge door, waiting to surprise his father.

Hand on heart, Fetid tried to catch his breath. "You shouldn't creep up on a man like that, Lance. I near burst an artery there."

"You're not my father," said Lance, holding aloft the dusty pages, loosely rebound by the black ribbon.

"Ah—erm—ah—erm –" Fetid took a cautious step back.

"My mother wasn't killed by the Little Nuns of St. Chuck Norris."

"Ah—erm—you see—that is to say –"

"You *made* me. It says it here. I'm a

flesh robot. Here – look at my picture. You made me evil."

Fetid backed up, right against the closed kitchen door. "Of course evil. What else? Son, sonny, my boy—evil is the only way to live." He gulped.

"That's not what these instructions say."

"Instructions schmucktions," Fetid said, his voice breaking mid-phrase, his plaintive gestures barely masking his desire to escape. "I built you big and strong too, didn't I?" Fetid pulled at the door handle but it was solidly locked.

"Looking for this?" Lance produced a key.

"You wouldn't harm your old Dad, would you?"

"No. I wouldn't harm my *old Dad*." Lance pulled a cleaver from its block and flung it, pinning Fetid to the door by his forehead. "But *you're* not my old Dad."

Lance flicked through the pages, thumbing his way to page seventy-four. "Toggle from Evil to Good."

These instructions he *could* follow: "Pull twice on left earlobe, once on nose and turn right nipple clockwise."

The goodness flowed into him, like the smell of fresh apples filling a room. He was no longer evil. There was, however, the small matter of a bloody corpse pinned to the kitchen door...

# 6 JOSHUA AND RUTH

"Sorry. Is anyone sitting here?"

"I'm thinking *no*. Unless they're very, very small."

"Um, right."

"Sit down. I was being sarcastic."

"S-s-sarcastic, yes. Very good."

I sat, my briefcase on my lap. She was very pretty. Not as pretty as the woman who makes my breakfast but pretty nonetheless.

Her dainty little hands tap-tapped on her laptop. My sister had hands like that. My sister owned a music player with white cords too, just like hers.

"Y-you like music, then."

She nodded.

"I like music."

She nodded.

"I like theme tunes. Do you like theme tunes?"

She pulled out a headphone. "I'm catching up on work here, sorry."

"That's very interesting. What do you work at?"

"In the city. I –"

"Oh, the city, I'm going there. Sorry. I interrupted you. I'm always doing that. Go on."

"I work for a hedge fund."

I smiled. Nice to be nice.

She replaced her headphone.

"I'm a handy gardener myself."

She nodded.

"I say, I'm a handy gardener myself."

She sighed and pulled out both headphones. "I'm very sorry. I really have to get this work done."

I patted my briefcase. "I have some work too."

Mother gave me the briefcase when I started school. I always liked the picture of Dan Dare and his friend, The Mekon.

"Do you like my tie?"

"Yes, erm, it's –"

"It was my father's. He was a philanderer."

"A what?"

"A philanderer."

I rubbed my palm three times on my slacks and extended my hand. "How rude of me. My name is Joshua."

Her eyes were a lovely blue. Reminded me of marbles.

She smiled. Often people don't smile. "Joshua, yes, that's a lovely name. I'm Ruth."

Her hand was soft, like chicken breasts, but warmer.

"And what, Joshua, do you do?"

"Everyday or on Sundays?"

"Everyday."

"Everyday, I mostly watch the news."

"And what do you do on Sundays?"

"I watch the news."

Ruth closed the lid of her laptop. "If you don't mind me asking, Joshua, what age are you?"

"I don't mind at all. I'm thirty-four. What age are you?"

"I'm twenty-three."

"We could never get married then. You're too young."

She put away her music player. "I have an older sister."

"Is she pretty, like you?"

"Yes, she's very pretty. She has a lunchbox just like yours. Has the A-Team on it."

"Lunchbox? Oh, you mean my *briefcase*. Di-de-di-di di-di-di. That's the A-Team."

"Yes it is."

"I don't like the A-Team."

I decided to be quiet for a while. People get spooked when I talk too much.

I opened my briefcase and counted the contents. I find it easier to count when I can point at the things. One. There was one thing in it. And it wasn't moving anymore.

"Where are you going, in the city?"

"You didn't look in my briefcase, just there, did you?"

"No."

"Good." I closed my briefcase and clutched it to my chest. "I'm going to...can I trust you?"

She moved close enough for me to be able to see the whites of her teeth. She had peppermint on her breath. "Yes. What's in the briefcase?"

I clutched it tighter. "No. It definitely isn't in here." I was sweating under my arms.

"Tickets, please!"

She fumbled in her handbag and produced her ticket. I showed him my brilliant card—it's a card that gets me everywhere for free because I'm brilliant.
The ticket collector smiled. "And where are you off to today, Joshua?"

I sat on top of my briefcase. "Nowhere, Toby."

"Well, you say hello to your Mum for me, won't you?"

"She's sleeping."

He winked. "So is this your girlfriend, Joshua?"

Ruth was all hands in the air. "I'm not like him—I mean *with* him."

"She's too young to be my girlfriend. She's twenty-three. She works with hedges."

"I'll catch you later, Joshua."

If he catches me I'll probably have to go to prison, I thought to myself. Then *I'd* be on the news. My Mum always told me that her heart belonged to my father. So I was taking it to him.

# 7 PASSENGER 57759, FIRST CLASS

Denise never thought she'd be married to a pirate. She never thought that her next door neighbour would be a troll who made bread from chicken bones (or any other sort of troll for that matter). But, how and ever, that was how things were and there wasn't much that she could change now. Didn't stop her from daydreaming, though. Didn't stop her from remembering the life she left behind when the ship sunk on that cold night.

"Arr," said Cap'n Blackflint as he ripped the leg from his duck dinner. "Tha' be great weather fer a corsair."

"Be it? I mean is it?" Denise sighed and wiped the table in slow circles with her dirty rag.

"Wha' be with ye, woman?"

"I don't know. I was just thinking about, you know, home."

Blackflint dropped the meat and for a moment she saw anger in his dark eyes. But the breath fell out of him and she saw something sad - there might even have been the makings of a tear in his eye.

"This be yer home, Denise. Here, with me. This be yer home. O, my darling, my beautiful red-haired queen, I wish that I could bring you home to your old life, to make you happy. It'd kill me but I'd do it to make you happy. You know tha', don't you?"

"I know." Denise folded her arms and gazed out the window of their wooden shack. Out there somewhere was England, her mother, her sisters Sophie and Constance and maybe even her father, if he survived.

"We had a garden. And a butler. He was called Jenkins. He used to sneak strawberries into my bedroom. I'd go to bed at night and there they'd be, in a great big bowl on my pillow."

Denise felt a hand on her shoulder. She placed her hand on his and smoothed the coarse skin in a slow caress.

"I'm sorry, Blackie. I should be okay about this now. I should be okay about the trolls, about the dragons, about everything. You've been so good to me, you really have. I don't think I would have survived if you hadn't found me on the beach that day. I should be more grateful."

Blackflint removed his hand and she heard him sit down again and begin to eat. She decided to change the subject.

"The trolls next door killed the chickens again."

He didn't answer.

"And that nest of dragons down at Devil's Spit will need to be sorted out before they get big enough to cause trouble."

Still no answer. The atmosphere had changed. He wouldn't even look at her. What had she said?

"I'll never mention it again. I promise."

He stopped eating.

"My love, there has been a terrible secret burning me heart out, these past ten years. It's dark as the devil's teeth—a secret that rots a man from the inside out."

"What? Oh, what is it, my love?" She rushed to him and on her knees she held his hand. "Here am I all a-worry about my strife, not thinking of you. What pain is it that ails you?" Her own sadness faded, usurped by the love she felt for her rescuer.

"Lass, stand up."

Denise stood up.

"Now take my cutlass. Take it now."

Denise took the sword and held it limply in her hand.

"After what I 'ave to say to you, when I tell you the secret, you may wish to drive tha' into my heart. I won't blame you if you do."

"But –"

"Keep it an' grip it tight, ye hear!"

Denise nodded. A deathly fear curdled in her gut. The voices of screaming passengers echoed in her mind, punctuated by the call of a young girl looking for her father.

Blackflint's praying hands pointed at Denise. "Ye hear me now. What I tell you is the truth…finally the truth. Many a year ago, a man told me of the magic of trollbones and dragonteeth. He told me that I could use that magic to go to another place an' find myself a bride of my own. I was lonely, Denise."

Denise didn't know what to say or to think but the fear began to course through her veins.

"I used that magic, my love, I used it. I came in a puff of purple cloud to a strange sea an'…an'…" Blackflint broke down.
Denise gripped the cutlass tight.

"If I'd only a-known. I swear I wouldn't a-done it, my love."

"Tell the story, Blackie. Tell the story."

Blackflint sniffed and rubbed his crimson sleeve across his nose. "I sees a great big ship, bigger than any I'd ever seen. In great letters I sees *RMS Titanic*. The magic man told me that was where I would find my bride."

Denise's knuckles whitened with the tightness of her grip.

"So I brought *The Buccaneer* behind an iceberg an' when the moment was right I used the magic to sink your ship. I took you right out of the sea, I did. An' I curse myself for it. I brought you here, to leave you on the beach…so that I could find you."

"YOU sunk the ship?" Denise pointed the cutlass at Blackflint. "You piece of shit. You black-hearted bastard."

"My queen – "

"Don't you 'my queen' me." Denise could hear her sanity crack. "I've cooked your dinners and cleaned up your rum-stinking clothes for ten years and you never once thought to tell me that *you* were responsible for me being here in the first place."

It happened before she could stop it: the blade pierced his throat, he gargled his own blood and then he was no more.

Denise never thought she'd kill a pirate. She never thought that she'd kill a troll, a dragon or a magic man either. But sometimes that's what you have to do, if you want to get home.

## 8 NO SPRING CHICKEN

"What's wrong, Grandad?"

"Don't be shocked if I get arrested, young man." The old watchmaker rapped his pipe on the oak table. "I'm a bad 'un." His lip curled with self-hatred. He hurled the pipe against the hearth where it failed to break so he stamped on it, causing it to fly towards me, ultimately missing by fractions of an inch.

"Oh, my boy, my young lad!" He cradled my head, as if I *had* been struck, rubbing my hair and sobbing. "You go now. You run. Run as fast as you can." Curiously, though he bade me escape, he now held me tighter. "Get as far away from your Grandad as you can. I'm nowt but trouble."

"No, Grandad. I'll not be leaving you."
I wrenched myself from his grip. "Tell me
what the problem is? We ... Mum or Dad or
Mr. Snickersby ... surely someone can help?"

"It's a hanging offence, me boy.
Hanging." He gestured to imitate a noose
being pulled. "We've been stealing time for
generations."

My jaw dropped. "How? What? Why?"

"Simple, me boy: it's all in the
springs."

"Springs?"

He leant forward and winked.
"Springs." He picked up his reserve pipe from
its stand. Drawing a long match from his tin,
he flicked it into flame with his yellowing
thumbnail. "Loose springs that hit the
minute mark a fraction late in the day, then
catch up in the night." The pipe stem clacked
between his dentures. "We're all in it
together, us watchmakers."

"B-b-but why?"

"The industrialists pay us to do it —
factory owners and such. That way the
workers toil harder and longer in the day
and have less time to themselves at night.
And they don't even know it."

"What about digital watches? Doesn't everyone use digital watches now?"

He dropped his pipe. Grandad's eyes glazed, a tear trickled down his weathered cheek. He turned his face, as if ashamed to look at me. "Gah! Dementia. Bloody dementia."

I placed my hand on his shoulder. "Oh, sorry, I forgot."

"That's ok, Barbara. Haddock jam baubles." He tousled my hair. I skipped back into the shop, still upset about Grandad's dementia but relieved that he wasn't going to jail.

## 9 HERR FLANGE'S NOODLE

Herr Flange ran his thin, grey, metal fingers along his handlebar moustache, tweaking the ends to an outrageous curl. "We preserved you in Pot Noodle form to protect you."

"I'm a Pot Noodle?"

"Yes, Agent Morgan, a Pot Noodle."

"I guess that's why my peas itch?"

"A common side-effect of the freeze-drying process."

"What year is it?"

"2525. A rather clement May morning."

"Three hundred years. Tell me, was Operation Chlamydia a success?"

"Not entirely. I'm afraid you were the only survivor."

"Francine? She's —"

"Dead. Yes. I'm so sorry, Agent Morgan, your file talks of how close you were."

"And Honest John?"

"Ahem, yes...he turned out to be not-so-honest-John."

"A traitor?"

"The worst kind. But our records show that he met with a very messy end."

"Bastard."

"Indeed."

"And now, why now? Why can I speak now?"

"You've been hydrated. I just have to get this sachet open and ...the damn thing is so fiddly...it says *tear here* but it just won't give. I'll go get a scissors."

"Wait, before you go, what's your name?"

"Flange, Augustus Flange."

"Augustus. What a strong name. Good for you. Do you have a special girl, Augustus?"

"Well, there is someone, a neighbour. We talk but I'm not sure she likes me, in that way, the way you mean."

"What's her name?"

"Giselle."

"French? How sweet? Is she beautiful, your Giselle? Tell me how beautiful she is."

"Ah, she is like a goddess in gossamer, a princess in pink."

"Go on..."

"Sometimes, when she doesn't know it, I watch her from across the park. She goes there every morning..."

"Don't stop."

"She goes there every morning to feed the pigeons. You don't want to hear this."

"I do. I do."

"She wears a pink dress—so pretty."

"Tell me of her neck—is it like porcelain?"

"It is. It is. I feel so ashamed."

"But why?"

"My thoughts are not always pure."

"No?"

"No. You see, she stirs something within me."

"Go on."

"My loins."

"Your loins?"

"My loins. I am not a young man. Have you read *Death in Venice*?"

"Many years ago."

"I am like Gustav von Aschenbach. I behold beauty and an irresistible innate passion takes control."

"Interesting."

"I'll get that scissors. We'll have the sauce stirred in and you'll be right as rain in a jiffy."

"No, Augustus, tell me more about Giselle."

"Are you sure?"

"The sauce can wait. Tell me about her face."

"Ah, she has the cutest button nose, and full cheeks around full red lips that glisten when she smiles. Her hair! It is boyish short, brown and messy—messy like her girlish giggles. I can see her now, laughing at my silly joke, her breasts tantalising as they bid for escape from her..."

"Go on...gnurf. Don't stop now...gnurf."

"Are you having a wank?"

"I'm not."

"You are, you're having a wank. The water's gone all clumpy."

"Anyway, I've finished now. Christ, that was some blockage. Three hundred years without cleaning out the pipes. Pop along and get that scissors, there's a nice chap."

"You can't just wank about my Giselle. You can't –"

"You're mixing me up with someone who gives a shit. Get the fucking scissors."

"Not sure if I want to now."

"Then don't."

"Maybe I won't. Maybe I'll leave you here. Maybe I'll pour you down the drain-"

"You wouldn't dare! Go on, I fucking dare you. No, I double-dare you. Pour me down the drain. Go on. You make me sick. Bleurgh. You make me want to hurl. You're dirt, you know that. Do you feel dirty?"

"Why are you being so cruel?"

"I don't know. I don't know. Gah, Augustus, maybe it's being freeze-dried for three hundred years, maybe it's the monosodium glutamate, or Francine or...or...I don't know. Can you forgive me? Can you ever forgive me, Augustus?"

"Yes. Yes, I think I can, Agent Morgan. I forget how much you have suffered, how much you gave so that generations could taste free air and drink in the elixir of democratic socialism. I can forgive you anything. I will get the scissors."

"Oh, and Augustus – "

"Yes?"

"When I'm re-constituted, can you introduce me to that girl of yours so that I can tell her what a swell guy you are?"

"It will be my pleasure."

\*

Augustus clacked his heel and marched out of the room, a skip inserting itself involuntarily into his joyous step.

Agent Morgan scratched his peas and thought—"Yeah, Giselle. I'm gonna bone the hell out of her."

## 10 GOOSEY CREEP
*For Sara*

"Great micturating donkeys!" exclaimed Constable Haywain before removing his helmet and vomiting therein. I closed my eyes and prayed to baby Jesus. This was worse than we had expected, far worse.

Even as I write now, years later, I cannot strike that image from my mind. My hand shakes as I grasp the silver handle of my tankard, my lips quiver as the warm ale floods down my throat.

I first came to Goosey Creep as a young student of dance, seeking out a rare country waltz, particular to that part of Dartmoor. It came as a great surprise to learn that dancing had been outlawed in this community some twenty years previous. A group of young people, a popular vagrant informed me, had been experimenting with ballet down an abandoned tin-mine when the joists gave way and all were lost. Most of the creative arts suffered in the backlash but the ultimate sanction was dealt to dance.

In this oppressive climate, I was most unwelcome. On the second morning of my stay, I awoke to a hammering on my bedroom door. I called out "hoi!" and "what ho!" but in the absence of a reply, I was forced to dress quickly and open the door. There before me, nailed to the wood, was a pair of flaming socks. When I enquired of my landlord the significance of this curious event, he replied—"A warning, that's all, a warning." The fact that his hands were charred and he was barefoot was not lost on me, so I moved lodgings that very day.

My next home was with Isadora Haywain, wife to the village constable. I met that lady in the most peculiar of circumstances. Her husband had arrested me for "skipping in a public place." I pleaded that I had tripped and that the weight of my bags had carried me forwards, perhaps *simulating* a skip but the Constable was not to be deterred from his charge. He led me straight to his house, which also served as the police station. Forced to strip under the pretext that I may be concealing objects of dance upon my person, I stood naked and alone in the scullery. Then I saw her. She wore a long flowing floral silk dress and a delicate peach scarf which floated like gossamer as she danced, yes *danced*, into the room. My eyes and my heart drank in this oasis in my desert. So distracted was I, that I failed to notice my shameful state of undress, until her open-mouthed gasp alerted me. She drew her scarf across her eyes, her see-through scarf. My hands reached to protect my modesty just as the Constable returned.

The Constable's face flushed something terrible: crimson to plum. When he asked her to leave, addressing her sternly as 'wife', I was shocked to learn that these two could be a pair. Before I had time to ponder this imponderable, he was in front of me, breathing into me, his eyes burning with what I thought was anger but a growing well of tears told me different: it was remorse, it was fear, it was sorrow. He demanded to know what I had seen but refused me answer, mumbling on in a one-sided conversation where he admitted that he was weak and that Isadora was obsessed with gyrating, with moving her body rhythmically, with the curse of dance.

Casting my clothes at me, he bade me stay with him one night, to be hospitable, and made me swear to leave Goosey Creep the next morning and never return. My options were few, the next carriage being a full twenty hours away, so I dressed and moved my bags to the small room in the attic where I would spend my last night in Goosey Creep. I wish now that I had run from that place, run for days and days.

My supper was modest and eaten in haste, as Isadora had the uncomfortable habit of stroking my thighs with her warm hands every time her husband's gaze was elsewhere. She would draw his attention to a particular part of the wall that might or might not have an unusual stain or a worrying crack and, without looking at me, her hand would travel from my knee to a place of which I cannot talk, for shame.

Tucked beneath my single sheet, I was confused about many things that night. When the door creaked open and a candlelit shadow entered, I feared, and hoped for, the worst. A whisper confirmed that it was not Isadora on a late-night foray, but the

Constable. Was she not here? That was his question. His countenance betrayed a sense of relief when I answered in the negative but his features quickly darkened. He pulled me by the arm, hoisting me out of bed. I was still fully-clothed.

We were out the door and bolting across the foggy moors within moments, he calling after me—"Goosey Creep Farm— that's where she is." Why did I follow? I suppose I felt some sympathy for this poor man and I will admit that I was curious about Isadora and where she might be. Was she dancing? Is that what happened at Goosey Creep Farm in the dead of night?

At the creaking gates my gay thoughts of midnight Morris dancing had departed. Morris dancing didn't smell like that.

Friend, having read this far, you can surmise that we reached the farmhouse door; you know that we opened it. You must desire to know what we saw. I will tell you—but never speak of this again.

Isadora was indeed behind that door, as was most of the village. But none were dancing. Friend, the shameful silence mixed with the expressions of horror and self-loathing. Oh! it is too much. In that remote farm, on the lonely moors of Goosey Creep, they were teaching kids how to smoke.

## 11 EXCERPT FROM *MEMOIRS OF AN ENGLISH GEISHA* BY ALBERT THRUPP *FOR QUACKER*

I will never forget the last time I met Edward Woodward, or Teddy, as we affectionately called him. We were both working on the set of *The Wicker Man*, him with his gritty acting hat on and me with my second-gaffer flat cap. It was the day we had filmed the now infamous Britt Ekland scene, where she writhed and danced naked against the wall of the room adjoining Sergeant Howie's. I remember Teddy wore brown pyjamas in that scene, the same ghastly brown pyjamas that he was wearing that last time we met. He had probably neglected to return them to wardrobe.

I had just finished my seventh gin and was about to neck a miniature bottle of Famous Grouse when the door burst open and the brown pyjama'd thespian stormed into the room.

"What are you doing in my bathroom?" he quipped. He was always quick-witted like that, coming up with witty one-liners such as "Stop feeling my bum," "If you touch me one more time I'll break your arm" and "No you cannot watch me undress."

"Your bathroom?" I replied, coyly adopting a faux-quizzical expression. "Whatever will we do?" I stood up, glasses and bottles crashing from my naked thighs, and offered my whisky bottle. "Fancy a bit?"

\*

I must have passed out then and probably bumped my head off something because I can remember no more of the conversation. The hospital staff told me that I was found the next day with several teeth missing, a broken nose and three broken ribs. Teddy, concerned for my health no doubt, must have carried me to the safety of the beach where I would certainly be discovered within days, at the very least.

Once my wounds had healed, I decided not to return to the set and left those remote Scottish islands for the comfort of home. I elected not to write to Teddy or to be within four-hundred yards of him, as the Chief Justice had suggested.

*

I was gutted to learn that he died 36 years later. We will never see his kind again. Indeed, just yesterday, in an exchange with Sir Anthony Hopkins I asked him what he thought of old Teddy and he replied, in the Welsh accent of his youth—"I don't know how you got in here but, trust me, this gun is loaded and I'm not afraid to use it."

Happy days. Halcyon days.

# 12 GAZEBAE

"This gazebo belonged to Queen Victoria," said Frobisher, absentmindedly polishing his sunglasses with a yellow chamois.

"I understand she had several gazebae," Frau Gruber replied, squinting into the summer sun.

Frobisher handed his black briefcase to her. That would be the job done. That *should* have been the job done. Operation GAZEBO *should* have ended there. The code phrases had been exchanged and the payload delivered. So why wasn't he walking away, going home to his own gazebo? Why then was he walking across the dewy grass, filling the very fresh footmarks of Frau Gruber?

To understand, we have to focus on the moment in the gazebo when their hands touched, the moment when their eyes met.

The hum of couples chatting, the intermittent clack of skateboard wheels smacking the pavement, the buzz of the honeybee, the rat-tat of a stilettoed lady wearing last night's dress and last night's make-up, a small child kneeling on the grass blowing on a dandelion clock: the summer context of St. Millicent's Gazebo at Chancery Park. A man with Brylcreemed hair stands in a pin-stripe suit, proffering a black leather briefcase to a pretty, blond woman in a white and red floral summer dress.

Frobisher felt the connection. In an instant her blue eyes had penetrated his thin-veneer, special-agent exterior and accessed his lost child interior. She must have felt it too: her smile as she spun away, the wink when she turned back to see him. She didn't need to turn back. Agents don't turn back—they walk on and never look back. But *she* did. She looked back. Why? He had to know.

The man steps down from the wooden gazebo onto the fresh cut grass. He walks with determined strides through the picnicking families and around the courting couples draped across each other like Henry Moore *vivants*. Any observer could deduce that he is following the blond woman in the white and red floral dress. She holds a black briefcase to her bosom and, any observer could deduce, she is in fear of something—something grave as death. Is she in fear of her pursuer?

Frobisher put his hand in his pocket and retrieved his Beretta. A man attacked her. A single shot rang out. She had seduced him into being her bodyguard. He had taken out her attacker, a Bolivian assassin, and now she was gone—forever. Forever?

\*

Frobisher's greying hair sympathised with the orange, brown and copper leaves of Chancery Park. Autumn was thinning the trees and thinning the crowds. No lovers on the grass, no children in the gazebo.

The gazebo. Every year, on the

anniversary of Operation GAZEBO he made this pilgrimage, this journey of disappointment. Frau Gruber had never reappeared. She had never been an agent, his superiors told him. She died in a bar brawl in Buenos Aires, a stranger uttered with his last breath.

A roadsweeper—brushes twirling, orange lights flashing—beep-beeps its way past the wooden gazebo. A man paces on the wooden boards, occasionally casting a glance out at the park, a glance with the very slightest tint of expectation. Across the grass walks a woman in a tan Mackintosh, wearing a floral headscarf and Chanel sunglasses. She stops, crushes her cigarette underfoot and surveys the gazebo.

"This gazebo belonged to Queen Victoria," she said.

"I understand she had several gazebae," he replied. This exchange had happened before. He could never be sure. He must not have hope.

"I'm so dreadfully sorry," she said, placing an arm on his shoulder. "That war...I'm so sorry. Beastly affair."

He turned, her hand leaving his shoulder in the process. His shoulder immediately mourned the loss. "I've come here every year."

"I'm so sorry. I didn't know. Life took over. Marriage, kids."

"I never married."

A tear came to her eye. "Never?"

"No."

She placed her hand on his shoulder and this time he didn't turn away. "*Gazebo*— I could never utter that word without thinking of you."

He laughed. "I worked in a garden centre when I was decommissioned. I know more about gazebos than any man should."

"Gazebos?"

"Yes, gazebos."

"Not gazebae?"

"No."

She sighed. "Have we wasted our lives, Henry?"

\*

A punk with a technicolour Mohican walks by the gazebo, a child in a warm, brown duffel coat holding his hand on one side and a rag doll on the other. Two crows peck at each other and at a rusty apple core. A blue balloon on a string drifts across the grass, childless and lonely. Inside the gazebo, a man with grey hair turns. A woman removes her sunglasses and wipes her eye. He takes her hand and draws her close. He says something. She smiles. They share a scintillating silence, drawing ever closer, never letting go. They kiss.

# 13 OLD RED

Losing my memory was nothing—I didn't know I'd lost it so it didn't matter much to me. I accepted that my name was Old Red and that I was homeless. It all made sense.

Getting my memory back—now that was something.

It started slowly. I was in the park, hanging out with Doc and Sniff, singing a Bob Dylan song to myself, shaking my cup, and a light went off in my head. It was the strangest thing. I had to chase the light. Didn't know why. But I had to.

"J!" I shouted. "There a *J* in it somewhere. Hey Sniff, there's a *J* in it."

"Quiet Red," he hissed. "The big dude

by the rubbish bin is watching us. He wants to steal my cheese." And he tapped his breast pocket with his gloved hand to let me know the cheese was there and that it was still safe.

Sniff was as good a friend as I could-a asked for but he was so caught up in protecting his cheese that sometimes he was no help at all.

So I knew there was a *J*. I didn't know why there was a *J*, or what it meant but I knew that it was connected to the light in my head and that I needed to follow it. I spent the whole day coming up with words that started with *J*.

"Hey Doc, d'ya think it might be Jesus?"

Doc had a stethoscope and prescribed hooch to us all. That was his joke. "You've got a bad case of septic underpants. I prescribe hooch. You've got pneumonia and I prescribe booze. You've got alcoholism and I prescribe alcohol. Sad thing is that Doc really was a doctor, in his old life.

"What might be Jesus?" asked Doc, spinning a Judy Garland CD on his finger.

"The *J*."

"Don't be a damn fool all your life,

Red. What would Jesus want with you?"
That hurt. Jesus is supposed to love everybody.

"What is it then? The *J.*"

"Cross my tongue with ethanol?"

I gave him a swig of my Red Biddy. Old Red Biddy—special recipe.

He coughed, inhaled sharply and spat. "Good stuff, Red. You've still got the apothecary knack."

"The *J*?"

"Of course," he said reverting to spinning the CD, "The *J.* Could it be John? Maybe your name is John."

"I don't feel like a *John.*"

"No, okay. That rules that out. What about *Jake*?" He held up one of my eyelids and peered into the eye with his ophthalmoscope. "Do you feel vaguely *Jake*-ish?"

I had to admit that I didn't. He moved to the other eyelid.

"Do you ever wake up feeling *Jeremiah* or *Jack*?"

That was it. "That's it!" I stood and unsteadily raised my bottle to the sky, to the gods. "I'm Jack." And, like a pineapple finally forced through a keyhole, a lump in me cleared and I knew everything. I remembered everything.

"I'm Jack freaking Dibbs!" I shouted, dancing, Doc joining me and sneaking a gulp of my drink. "I'm Jack freaking Dibbs and I'm from Kettering!" It had started to rain but that didn't stop us. Sniff joined in, one hand on his pocket so his cheese wouldn't jump out. We were all screaming "I'm Jack Dibbs!" as the rain washed the dirt from our hair into our wet-dog smelling coats. We knocked back the last of the special recipe Red Biddy.

"I'm Jack freaking Dibbs, from Kettering, and my wife . . ." I was *married*? I was married!

We locked arms and danced in a circle singing "Mr. and Mrs Jack freaking Dibbs."

"I'm Jack freaking Dibbs, from Kettering, and my wife and kids . . ." I had kids? Yes! A boy and a girl: Charlie and Zoe, without the umlaut.

We locked arms and went counterclockwise this time. "Charlie and Zoe, without the umlaut. Yeah, yeah without the umlaut.'

"I'm Jack freaking Dibbs, from Kettering, and my wife and kids..."

I stopped dancing.
"...died in a fire that I caused."

\*

I've been trying to lose my memory ever since.

## 14 MATTY UNFINISHED

Matty scratched his head.

> *"Stake out my meagre domain,*
> *Seed with hope and pray for rain,*
> *Say it comes not?*
> *Sow again my plot."*

His mother's verse whispered in a distant corner of his distracted mind. He tipped his cigarette into the empty silver milk churn and sighed. From the crooked doorway of his whitewash cottage he could smell the salt air of the Atlantic as it whipped past the leaning trees. Out there, beyond the scrub hills and the limestone fields, along the rocky coast, side by side with the porpoise swim—out there was a woman. He didn't know her name but he would find her today.

Matty stubbed the cigarette out and pocketed the half-chance that was left of it; the cold, flowerless kitchen awaiting. He was given to groaning as he sat, his knees, at seventy-five, needing a little encouragement. Rounds of bread and butter for breakfast, a cup of tae strong enough to trot a horse on and sweeter than cake. His hands, he observed as he poured, were not beautiful – they were tanned with sun and dirt, thick and coarse to be fit for work. They were not beautiful.

"Arra, would you ever have a hand like this in yours?" he whispered.

He bit down on the buttery bread and in slow chews took in the quiet of the small kitchen. She might want to paint this, he thought. She might want to paint it yellow. He'd have to change the ware – new cups and plates and knives and forks and spoons. The table wobbled under his elbow: she'd want to change that too. The oak was grey and pitted with holes. The room would look that much brighter with a red Formica top. He tapped the sole of his shoe on the stone floor. That'd have to go too.

"The dirt of that," he mimicked in a high-pitched voice as he wiped the dishes with the cloth of ages. "Sure the dishes are cleaner than the cloth!"

\*

Every year in September he travelled to Lisdoonvarna in the County Clare. And every year he returned alone. This year, his match would be made – he could feel it in the rise of excitement that fluttered in his belly and his bones. The square in that small village would be all decked out with dour men in dark coats and drunk men in huddles. There would be a woman there, standing alone. That'd be her.

And so the ceremony that prefigures the Lisdoonvarna Matchmaking Festival began for Matty in earnest. A white enamel bowl, filled from the warmer of the two taps, welcomed his hands in a flurry of lather.

"Did you know Mar-y? Did you know Mar-y?" he sung softly, in a faraway air. "From Tipp-erary. From Tipp-erary." His hands embraced in the soap and the hardness melted away. He lathered his face. Then in slow, measured razor glides, his tanned chin reappeared from beneath the milky foam. The sound of the scrape of a true razor, like the smell of a pint from an honest bar, cannot be faked.

From the bottom drawer of his battered dresser he produced, with a flourish, a white Donegal linen cloth. He laid it across the table, taking care over each corner and crease. A small Belleek vase he placed on the centre, bearing the wildflowers from that mornings' harvest.

One last look in the tiny circular mirror. He tilted his hat on the Kildare side, allowed himself a playful smirk and then righted it. Out now, out now into the world, he thought to himself, as he shouldered open the small front door.

Outside, Mrs. Spencer, the blue-uniformed postmistress, herself in her seventies, pulled up in her green van.

"Where are you off to now, Matty, all dressed up like de Valera?"

"I'm off to Lisdoonvarna to get myself a bride and a new dishcloth." And Matty tipped his hat and gambolled down the narrow boreen and into the rest of his life.

*"Stake out my meagre domain,*
*Seed with hope and pray for rain,*

*Say it comes not?*
*Sow again my plot."*

## 15 MY HIRSUTE HERO

*As told by Gerald Fring to Thaddeus Lovecraft.*

"I first met Noel Edmonds back in the summer of 1982. *Saturday Swap Shop* had just been canned and he was foraging for grubs and berries behind the shed at the foot of my garden. His trademark beard and groovy hairdo were in tatters; his glasses were held together by a grubby plaster and his duffle coat smelt like a wet dog that had been sick on itself. I must have stepped on a twig because as I approached he dropped a bottle of Lucozade and began to back off.

"Noel, sh! Noel, it's okay. I won't hurt you."

His face was all twitchy and he backed off a bit more. To my surprise, as I moved my hand slowly towards his greasy mane, he bared his teeth and hissed. Being skilled in negotiation and facilitation, I kept eye-contact and purred slightly, allowing my hand to continue towards his bedraggled beard.

"That's right, Noel. I'm your friend." I stroked his beard slowly and gently until the hissing died down. He was still twitchy but I knew that the greater part of the battle was over: he did not fear me anymore.

Grasping his hand firmly in mine, I led him towards the back door of my house. I could feel him tug away as we moved to cross the threshold but I stroked his beard again and he relaxed. Once inside, I bade him sit at my kitchen table and I boiled the kettle, to make a nice hot cup of Bovril - Noel's favourite.

"Noel," I said, "you shouldn't carry the worries of the world on your shoulders like that. Look what it has done to you already."

He didn't reply. Noel was a frightened little child in a grown man's beard. He grunted, twitched and began to pick his nose. How terrible it was to behold one so great fallen to such a base existence. I handed him his meaty Bovril.

I did think of getting out the phone book and ringing Maggie Philbin or Cheggers to see if they would come and rescue their friend but in my heart of hearts I knew that they were part of the problem. No, my job there and then was to be with him, to *hold* the silence – nothing more, nothing less. He drank with far less grace than one would expect of a television celebrity but then who is to say that the measure of a man is in how much of his beverage he keeps off his shirt? Certainly not I.

"Noel, would you like to stay here with me for a while or is there somewhere that I can bring you?"

I knew that my wife would probably object to a houseguest – she doesn't share my Samaritan spirit – but the offer needed to be made, as a Christian duty.

Noel shook his head and a small beetle was released onto the table top. He crushed it with his able fist.

"Is that 'no' as in you have nowhere to go or 'no as is you don't want to stay here?"

Love and gratitude are very complex but when he punched me in the mouth I could feel the love and gratitude like an electric current zinging in the air. Holding the place where my lower front teeth once were, guiding the blood down my chin, I gazed once more at this demi-god with renewed admiration. Well, I suppose you know most of the rest of this story as it has been detailed so frequently in *Hello!* and *Readers Digest* but I'll tell it to you again. Noel took a long piss on my floor, removed a box of cornflakes from the cupboard and then left using the front door.

*

I didn't see him again for, oh, twenty years or so. I was in a very low place when next we met. My wife had left me and my business, an internet start-up selling wardrobes and manure, had failed. I think it was a train station or a bus stop, I can't be too sure, these details are a touch fuzzy, but I knew it was Noel the second I laid eyes upon him. *Noel's Houseparty* had recently been cut from the BBC schedule and he was talking to an old lady about a prospective financial transaction. I believe he was looking for a small loan to tide him over until Cash Converters opened in the morning. The old lady, obviously not a fan, began to shout obscenities at him and to strike him with her brolly. Are the likes of her really better off in the community?

"Noel! It's me! Remember?" I flashed a gappy-toothed smile. Little did I know that right there and then this beautiful bearded angel was going to change my life forever.

*

When I came to in the hospital later on, the policeman informed me that Noel had picked up a bicycle and literally beat me to a pulp with it. Even now as I strain to drink my dinner from the tube and dream of what it might be like to walk again, I can't help but reflect on my hirsute hero and how he touched my life in a way that only he could. Noel, wherever you are, I know you are thinking of me."

*Author's note: Alas, my friend Gerald died last year when, mistaking a chainsaw for a piece of cheese, he cut his own head off at the mouth.*

## 16 A VERY SUBURBAN HAUNTING

"I think he may be dead," I said.

"Are you sure?" said Roger, the man sitting opposite me.

The other twelve members of the committee had fallen silent, having forgotten their argument about the hedge-cutting on the crescent and the weed-filled potted plants on the green, and focused their now rapt attention on the grey-faced man at the head of the boardroom table.

As if in answer to Roger's question, the grey-faced head lolled forward. Graham Hardchester was dead.

That, my friend, is how it came to pass that I, Millicent Granger-Hewitt, became the first female chairperson of the Greater Grimley Residents' Association. It was also, I can see now, the catalyst for the hauntings.

*

The funeral was the very next day, as the Hardchester Family had a very full diary for the rest of the week and that was the only available slot. The eulogy, fittingly, was delivered in Afrikaans, a language that Graham had suffered from in his later years. The family lined up outside to receive the mourners and swap email addresses. Graham had kept himself to himself mostly, so none of his family were known to us. I learned that he had three brothers, no sisters, a sister and another brother. And we shook the hands of all six as we passed along the line.

"Sorry for your loss," I'd say. "MillicentGH123@gmail.com."

And they'd nod solemnly and say 'such_and_such@domain.com' and I'd move on to the next. However, the last person in the line, Archie Hardchester, pulled me close, as if he knew me.

"I know," he whispered, "that you're

probably wondering why I pulled you close, as if I knew you."

Could he read my mind?

"You have heard the rumours of my arrest for frotteurism, have you not? Well, that is only partly to blame. I must tell you that Graham talked many times of you, of how you helped him with the committee. I must also tell you that, the day before he died, he consumed something mysterious that will undoubtedly result in mysterious outcomes."

"Thank you," I uttered, not sure where to look. After a moment he sighed and released me from his grip.

Later that night, when I returned home, I looked up frotteurism in the dictionary and burnt my clothes on the lawn.

*

Two weeks later, the residents had convened an EGM to elect a new chairperson and to question whether the apostrophe in the title would go before or after the *s*. I was surprised to be nominated as chairperson, especially by Roger, whose advances I had spurned not five minutes before the meeting.

"No, I won't touch it," I'd said. "Put it away before anyone sees."

He put his gun back in his shoulder holster and asked me if I would like to go to the cinema with him, on account of the fact that his wife didn't understand him. She was from Bogotá and spoke no English.

I replied, indignant, "Of course I will not go with you to the cinema. You, sir, are a married man." I buttoned up my blouse and left him there to put his shoes and socks back on and ponder his own feculence.

At the meeting, the vote was unanimous. I was to be chairperson. My first decision was to remove the apostrophe entirely from the Residents Association. My second decision was to ask that we re-commission the gardener to replant the azalea garden. As these very words left my lips a chill wind passed through the room, tussling with the net curtains and extinguishing the candles.

"Woooo!" said a ghostly voice.

"Since when did we have candles at committee meetings?" said Mr. Gherkin, the tall man at the end of the table with the curly-black mutton chops and the stovepipe hat.

"Woe! Oh, woe!" said the ghostly voice.

"Seriously," said Mr. Gherkin, "with

all these net curtains that's got to be a fire hazard."

"Gherrrkinnnnn!" said the voice. "Beeeee quiet you little man!"

Something happened to Mr. Gherkin that very instant. Years later he would claim that it was indigestion and a touch of cholera but I knew that something spectral had reached into his soul and shown him hell. He turned a shade of pea-green before sobbing uncontrollably and ultimately collapsing in a foetal heap.

"Woe! Oh woe!" repeated the ghostly voice.

Mrs. Stokes, who ran the B&B at No.75, a respected state-registered medium, chose this moment to speak. "I believe there is a spirit in the room," she said, her arms spread out as if to block a rugby tackle from both sides. "And I believe that it is a restless spirit, recently passed. None other than that of Mr. Hardchester!"

"Wooo!" said the ghostly voice. "You are spooooottttt onnnn."

And to make a point, I believe, the spirit caused the computer screen on the end wall of the room to go into sleep mode.

"Oh!" said Mr. Gripthrottle, rubbing

his thighs. "Do something else, do something else."

"Sh!" said Mrs. Stokes. "Spirit! Spirit! What ails you? What is stopping you from passing to the other side?"

"Azaleas! Azaleas!" boomed the spirit. The lights flashed on and off, Mr. Twink's bowtie mysteriously spun and all the water in the room became inexplicably tepid. "Don't plant azaleas!"

Now was the time for leadership, for clear thinking. "Should we plant fuchsias instead?" I offered to the ether.

"Yes," came the macabre reply.

"It's agreed then," I said, "We shall plant fuchsias in place of azaleas this year." With that, the candles came to life, the computer screen flickered on, the net curtains did nothing and Mr Gherkin burped.

Mrs Stokes stood. "The spirit is now at peace. He has passed. Mr. Hardchester has passed." Her eyes rolled in their sockets and she fainted.

"I hereby bring this meeting to a close," I said, "and we shall meet next in four weeks to discuss the erection of a statue to Larry Hagman."

That night, dear friend, and for no good reason, I went home and burnt my clothes on the lawn.

# 17 AN EXISTENTIALIST TAKE ON POST-WAR CONSUMERISM
## *For Painkillers*

With his tartan handkerchief, Denzel Funtengast wiped the condensation off the glass of his brass goggles. This was more out of habit than out of necessity—the habit of occupying his mundane conscious brain so that his eccentric and brilliant sub-conscious could wrangle with a troublesome problem.

"So you have no antimony, whatsoever?" he said.

"None. What-so-ever," replied the Brylcreemed shopkeeper, drumming his fingers on the counter, keeping beat with the syllables.

"No splonge levers?"

"Nope."

"Any immoculator grease?"

The shopkeeper sighed wearily, twisting the ends of his handlebar moustache. "Sir, I daren't try to guess what an immoculator is or what is done with it once greased, but no. Now kindly move on, unless you have some genuine business to transact."

Denzel surveyed the premises. This was a bit of a bind.

"This is a bit of a bind," he said.

The shopkeeper shrugged.

Denzel withdrew his shabby pocket book and thumbed through the inky pages, stopping on a page that was jammed margin to margin and beyond with mathematical formulae. He realised that he would now have to recalibrate his vectors.

"I'll have to recalibrate my vectors, you know," he said, pulling out his stubby pencil and licking the tip.

The shopkeeper smiled like a man who hadn't quite mastered the art and leaned surreptitiously towards a black Bakelite phone. "Whitehall 1–2 1–2," he whispered.

Denzel's nib snapped. "Damn it, man.

Damn the very socks of it." His calculations pointed to one thing and one thing alone. "My calculations point to one thing and one thing alone—I cannot now complete my trip."

"Yes he's here right now, he's —" the shopkeeper stopped, mid-sentence. "Ah," he said into the receiver. "I think, Constable, that I may have been a little astray in my conjecture. I can take it from here. Yes. Sorry for bothering you." Replacing the receiver, he addressed Denzel. "Sir, this *trip*, where would it take you?"

Denzel stepped back, placed his hand on his hips and laughed. "Ha! Why the Moon, of course. Where else?"

"Where else, indeed," said the shopkeeper. "I think I see what our problem is."

"Yes?" said Denzel, curiosity piqued.

"Can I ask you," said the shopkeeper, "What sort of vehicle you will be using to complete this journey?"

"One of my own creation: *The Indubitable*. The finest example of steam-powered engineering in the Empire—seven tonnes of gleaming cogs, spindles, levers, throckets, sprockets and dials."

"Right there: there's your problem."

"Where?"

"All that sprockets and cogs and steam nonsense. You're quite clearly in the wrong short story."

"Wrong story?"

"Yes. You are a *steampunk* character. This story is an existentialist take on post-war consumerism. "

Denzel blushed. "Oh, I'm so embarrassed."

"Don't be, sir. It could happen to anyone. I had a Roman Centurion in here last week, looking for directions to the forum. Had to tell him it was a cinema now."

"So what do I do?"

"Wait, I suppose."

Denzel reverted to rubbing his goggles with his tartan handkerchief. He paced the shop, looking at the merchandise, pulling a jam jar off the shelf here and a box of soap flakes off the shelf there, reading the labels, nodding and smiling, nodding and smiling. He opened a jar of hair ointment and smelled the unctuous contents, ran his fingernails along an array of tortoise-shell combs, shook a box of tea and read a recipe from the back of a custard tin.

"This is taking forever," he said.

"It is," replied the shopkeeper. "I imagine that it is as painful to read as it is to write."

"Quite," said Denzel.

"Quite," said the shopkeeper.

# Fin

# 18 THE IRRESISTIBLE STORY OF HOW YOU DIED

*For Wildwords*

On the corner of Short and Long Street is a derelict house with a small, circular, blue plaque on the wall. Passers-by ignore the run-down, roofless property—except to comment how the building should be razed to the ground, because of the tramps and the rats and Weil's disease and the empty cider cans. The lettering on the plaque, almost as unloved as the residence itself, is all but worn away.

If you managed to climb over the security fence that the council erected after the accident, then you would first have to negotiate the laceless trainers, some with poo in, some without. Then you would have to avoid the six-foot hole in the ground that locals think was intended as a triad grave. Finally, you would want to side-step the cats' graveyard, a space in the front garden where a lazy council worker had been tossing road-kill. Only then would you be standing beneath the blue plaque, and only then would you be able to squint and make out the letters.

> Urbania Dunstable
> Inventor
> Was born here in 1921
> And died here in mysterious circumstances in 1975

If then, piqued by the intrigue and brimming with the courage of a person who had successfully avoided seven laceless, poo-filled trainers, you decided to respond to your natural curiosity, to your innate desire to seek closure in all things, then you would have begun the journey that would end your life.

Scared? You should be.

What, you ask, would have happened had you knocked on the door of the next house on Long Street or the adjacent house on Short Street? Seems logical as your next port of call, doesn't it?

If you were to rap gently on the red oak door of No. 2 Long Street, a woman in a floral house-coat would answer, one eyelid closed shut to hide the missing eyeball.

"I was just in the area," you'd say, "and I saw that blue plaque."

"Blue plaque, you say?" she'd say.

And before you'd had a chance to nod or point or scream, she'd have shot you in the forehead with the very nail gun that caused her to lose her left eye. She's like that, the widow at No. 2 Long Street. She would have dragged you from the porch, checking left and right, brought you to the shed at the back of her garden and then skinned you.

*

So, what about No.1 Short Street, I hear you say, as you check over your shoulder for axe-murderers and sex-fiends? Well what about it? Are you *still* curious? Have you not learned your lesson? Very well...

If you were to knock assertively on the door of No.1 Short Street, you would first be taken by the knocker itself, which, you would realise to your disgust, was dripping with blood. It might take a moment or two before you would understand that the blood was your own. A rusty spike, coated in a numbing agent, shot right through your hand the second you touched the knocker. The door would then open and a thin man with jaundiced eyes and a withered arm would emerge.

"Can I help you?" he'd say, his withered arm suddenly caught by an unexpected gust of air and thrown up in an involuntary wave.

"I appear to be bleeding," you'd reply, as the numbing agent wore off.

"Oh dear," he'd say, his thin, knobbly tongue running over his thin, parched, chapped lips. "Come in. I have some arnica around here somewhere. "

He'd bring you into his kitchen and you'd ignore the smell, just to be nice. You would be struck by the metres of fly-paper hanging from the ceiling. You might even start counting the flies on one strip and stop before you'd get to a hundred, stop because what he is rubbing on your cut is not arnica, stop because the expression on his face, the angle of his grin, is just south of twisted and well north of insane. You'd scream. You'd bang your free hand on the Formica-topped table—of course you would, who wouldn't? What he was rubbing on your open wound was a snake, a thin, venomous snake with purple and red scales and eyes as jaundiced as their owner. Of course, you'd be paralysed in seconds. Death wouldn't come quickly though, and you can be sure that Mr. No.1 Short Street would have some sexual peccadilloes that he's been aching to try out.

*

Right now, you are thinking *why did I have to climb that fence? Why couldn't I have simply walked past and continued on to my job as a blah at the blah-blah-blah.* You move uneasily in your seat, conscious that a few moments ago there was a noise upstairs that you cannot explain. It could have been a tree tapping on a window or maybe something in the attic settling and falling— but you know it wasn't.

Yet still, despite the faint scent of ammonia that is filling your room, you are consumed by Urbania Dunstable and the *mysterious circumstances* in which she lost her life. Who was she? How did she die?

When you go to bed tonight you will sleep for two hours, whereupon a one-eyed, one-armed bastard son of No.1 Short Street and No.2 Long Street will wake you, tell you who Urbania Dunstable was and show you how she died. Then he will take the laces out of your trainers and poo in them.

# 19 EXCERPTS FROM *THE HOLY BOOK OF NIGEL*

*Author(s) unknown*
*As copy'd in earneste by one Thomas Hardy.*

Yea, verily, it is with a heavy heart that I sit down this eve to write this work. It falls to me as the last keeper of the last secret of the known and unknown universes to journal that secret, now that my wife and daughters have been slain by the one they call Tom Fielding. I was tending to my gazelles and the sun was setting in the east or west or whichever took its fancy that day when there came a rustle near the arse-end of the field.

"Ageep, ageep!" I called out, in the common parlance of my kind, hoping to startle whatever lay in those quarters, amidst the flowers of the jimjombles and the berrywongles. I thought it might have been a night-shark or a stuttering gobshite foraging for eggs but to my utter, wretched dismay it was not. I curse mine own eyes for what they saw, for 'twas a sight that no living man or beast should ever behold. Indeed, were it not for the opium and the camphor I might have fainted on the spot. What I saw was the unsheathed bum of the one they call William Shakespeare, a near neighbour of mine, and it was rutting with a ferocity that caused the air around to fill with steam. Imagining that The Bard was simply indulging his nocturnal cravings, I thought to return to the feeding of my herd but my eye was caught by the twinkle of moonlight on a burnished bracelet. It was the jewellery of Marlowe, no doubt, the singular jewellery of Marlowe. I had not thought Shakespeare to be so particular in his choice of mate but this came as a shock to me, both being sworn enemies, since a long-ago dispute over the exact weight of Denmark. It was at that very moment, as I stood transfixed by the bracelet, I realised that Marlowe was already deceased and that Shakespeare was possessed of something most evil. Perhaps it was the axe embedded in his back, or the knife through his neck, or maybe the distinctive red glow of his eyes. Something was very definitely awry.

{The three pages following were illegible, being smeared with blood and soot. TH}

and even the bats themselves wept. I buried my family 'neath the woebegone tree and retired here to determine my next course of action. And this is what I have resolved to do: to document the Universe since the beginning of time and to present for posterity the last secret.

To begin: In the beginning there was nothing. This was succeeded by generations of different nothings, each with their own unique abyssal depth and infinitely tiny emptiness. Then there was a nothing which surpassed all other nothings by the simple expedient of being something. It was not much—a nothing that smelled faintly of mint—but it was something and that, in the realm of everything, mattered. It was succeeded by a nothing that tasted of burnt garlic and, in turn, that was succeeded by a nothing that could have been described as sounding like a bell.

{What followed may have been the wanderings of a madman. Methinks the opiates overruled the inks. I have expunged the following twenty-seven pages. TH}

And lo! There was The Word! And the word begat the truth. And in each word a rock was born and on to each rock a seed was thrown by a hand unknown, the first hand. A song was sung, the murmur of a shepherdess thinking of the men on the hunt and the taste of goat's milk. The harmonics disturbed the ether and the seed split, a root grasping for a crevice that it found. Life began: a green shoot hungrily searched for the sun.

*

Verse 27:12

The people of Yashob, dwelling near the caves of Al-Mun-Humraan, where they existed on a diet of innuendo and supposition, were the inventors of the concept of subtraction: before Mak-mul-tabaa, the father of subtraction, people were only aware that adding numbers together created a bigger number. It was Mak-mul-tabaa who showed the naïve that by eating a chunk of bread the loaf did indeed become smaller, by killing one ox one could very easily calculate that there were fewer oxen in the field, by deflowering one virgin, the numbers of chaste women diminished. Mak-mul-tabaa was slain by Kha-mul-Hajii—for he was the original owner of the bread, the ox and the chaste daughter.

Verse 28:15

And the woman of many hairs descended from the mountain to be with her people again. It is said that she revealed much of what the future would hold but chief amongst that she proclaimed that 'though man will put another man on the moon with great fire, he will not know how to dry his hands or pick up lint efficiently off the carpet until the blessed one they will call Dyson shows him the way.' It came to pass that a boy was born and he was named Dyson. He died in a freak gardening accident and everyone agreed that he probably wasn't the Dyson she was referring to.

Verse 31:28

It was written and then it was erased and re-written some years later that there will come into our world a boy. He will not glow like a molten tangerine, nor will he float like a floaty thing, nor will he sparkle like a sparkly thing. No! He will be without these three attributes that the Oracle Khafaled had once sworn blind that the boy would possess. We know now, through the wisdom of time, that the Oracle Khafaled was too fond of the fermented wasp; that he was prone to lying outright; that his third eye was drawn on and that the frenzies which he affected when he claimed to be channeling the gods were, in truth, symptoms of the early onset of palsy.

Yet, another came forward, and he smelt of dandelions on a wet autumn morn, and he was called Dandelion on a Wet Autumn Morn by the villagers, and he did write, for I have the said writings before me now, that a boy will come into a world and he will be a bridge, a portal, a gateway to another place. And he was asked, for the villagers were curious, "Where is this other place?" And Dandelion on a Wet Autumn Morn did point skyward and say "I don't know."

The villagers all looked up and were temporarily blinded by the second of the three suns, whereupon Dandelion on a Wet Autumn Morn did take liberties with the vestments of three of the least uncomely maidens. The punishment meted out by the villagers was swift. Having endured all but three chapters of Gulliver's Travels, Dandelion on a Wet Autumn Morn passed into a sleep that lasted seven minutes and a year. Upon his revival, he bade the eldest of the villagers to come hither. Gnarl, for it was he who carried the most years in his pocket, came forward. The message that was relayed to him turned his grey hair black and withered his leg on the spot. After that, the other villagers were not at all keen on hearing the message. Gnarl survived for just thirty moons, constantly muttering the same phrase over and over—'le sang de lonfont. Apportay le sang a la foy cat-orze.' Dandelion on a Wet Autumn Morn lived well into his dotage, but never spoke again, having had his tongue ripped out by suspicious villagers.

The boy did not feature in the literature until several centuries later when the Psalms of Hickbert did make mention of—
"The boy, who hath not been written but carried in the air on Gnarl's tongue, hath the unctuous liquor running in his veins that will free us from our bondage. Fear not the gimpy storms that puck and shrew. Take ye the blood and cast it forth!" Hickbert wrote only this psalm and one other on the topic of shadows and their propensity for sinning. "Has not the shadow hands with which it can grope other shadows? Has not the shadow organs of night-time mischief with which it can beget other, smaller shadows? I say to you now, that your shadow is accursed and you must regard that dark spectre as thine gravest enemy: for who is to know, where the shadows go at night and what lascivious acts they might be perpetrating, under cover of darkness?" Hickbert, it was recorded in the Journale Ecclesiasticus, was strangled by his own shadow, or his wife, the case for either never having been satisfactorily proven.

The great seer, William the Blind, ten minutes later did write—

"It is interesting, is it not, that we are so eager to find this boy and voyage to this other place when we know naught of what ill we may find there. It reminds me of the story of the man who lived beside a great mountain. Every day, as he tended his meagre plot, he wondered what might lie on the other side of yon mountain. He had barely enough nettles to feed his family and his beetles were dying of tuberculosis. His wife would chide and chasten him—'Fool. There are no nettles over yon mountain, no fat beetles. Do your work here and feed your family. Desist from thine bendy dreams.' It was one chasten too many, for the following morning he set out, with his favourite shoe, for the other side of the mountain. He braved the heat, the cold, the rain, the snow and the shingles, reaching the top of the mountain in seventeen short years. The other side being downwards, he did tumble for most of it, when he was not skidding or sliding, and he made that portion of his journey in just under twenty years. Lo! He was an old man when finally he came back to report that the other side of the mountain was naught but a wasteland. And during his absence his wife had remarried, his children had also remarried and his brother was now a goat.

'So,' he lamented, 'for the sin of my greed, I have missed four weddings and my dear brother, through shame, has become ungulate.'"

William, being fickle, did then ponder a moment, in a written way, and report—

"Of course, there is the tale of Damaskin, son of Charbrick, who lived beside a lake—I think his story ended differently. I seem to remember something about finding virgins and gold."

And those close to William whispered—

"If you are blind then how come you can write?"

Whereupon, William pointed skywards and vanished, or left.

Verse 37:1

Morgan of the large hands was always in demand, come the harvest, or when livestock fell into the river. In the winter, he was scorned by his neighbours, who grew tired of broken crockery and random groping. Year after year, he would be stoned in the town square for crimes against plates and bottoms, only to be celebrated in the fields come spring. Year after year, he would endure the peaks and troughs of his social relations until one winter when he became weary and crushed the entire village under his boot. I may have neglected to mention that Morgan was a giant.

Verse 39:11

In the land of Smorg a cult gained a foothold—The Cult of The Second Sun. For twenty years or seventeen fathoms, this mystic abomination did propagate its heresy, growing its cohort to several thousand adherents. The chief tenet of the cult was that 'All men shall be good to all men.' The secondary tenet was that the second sun was the only true sun and that the other two suns were the work of the devil. Adherents were forbidden to wear shoes or eat pastry.

One day, into the land of Smorg, came a stranger from a foreign land. This man wore the stitched skins of avocados beneath his soles and he baked breads with molasses. The people were concerned. They consulted Gitar, their high priest.

"This man," they said, "says that he

wears not shoes nor does he eat pastry. But, great Gitar, we're not so sure. Are avocados shoes? Is sweet bread not like pastry?"

"My people," spake Gitar. "All men shall be good to all men. So it is written, so it shall be."

The townsfolk returned to their holes in the ground, unsatisfied by the answers of their master. There was great shaking of heads and the people did not rest well that night, owing to the shaking of heads. The following day, as it was the only day of the year that the second sun outshone the two others, a sacred day in the Smorg liturgical calendar, a special decree was made by the High Priest of Smorg to celebrate the day.

"That foreigner," the High Priest decreed, "shall henceforth be redefined as a chest of drawers."

And, as the tenets did not forbid it, the chest of drawers was burnt.

*

Verse 41:2

Bethlezekial, daughter of Shoom, son of Gabbidon, found herself alone on the mountain of Arak. She had been herding worms into the early morning when a great

115

fog did descend, separating her from her three sisters. Appealing to the god of the grasses, she knelt down and sacrificed a stone, following the ritual of her people. She died four days later of apoplexy and chills. Her body was found by a local tax-collector who immediately recognised the bangle that she wore at her feet, for she had been his playmate as infants in the field. Kneeling, he too sacrificed a stone to the god of the grasses. Being weak in the livers, the distress affected him greatly and he fell instantly to his death. The parents of Bethlezekial and of the tax-collector wailed and ululated upon hearing the news of the passing of the young lovers.

"If only," Shoom lamented, "they had more stones."

# 20 MONKIES, PONIES AND ASSORTED LEGAL TENDER

Cyril scrunched up his nose, his two long, front teeth exposed in the expression, rendering him more rat-like than heretofore imaginable.

"I won't take a monkey," he said, rubbing his long, stubbly chin with one hand and weighing up the vase with the other. "But I'll give it ye for a giraffe." His narrow eyes focused on me with the cold assuredness of a man who not only knew his slang for money but who knew that a type like me would wet himself if confronted by a type like him down a dark alleyway or in a crowded pharmacy.

I was way out of my depth.

"A giraffe?" I offered, pulling my Crombie coat closer to me and rubbing my hands together to stave off the cold. "Wouldn't a...em...gazelle and three score be closer to the mark? I mean to say there's a chip there, on the rim." A *gazelle*? Would I get away with it?

"A chip?" he said, his eyes widening in mock disbelief and disbelieving mocking. "A chip, says the Eton boy in the funeral coat." He turned his head to the next stall-holder, the fat, bearded man who operated the second-hand book table. "A chip?" The fat, bearded man continued to pick at his teeth but offered Cyril a knowing shrug.

"That, my boy," said Cyril, "is a flaw. It is a maker's mark. I'll have you know that in Japan this kind of blemish would DOUBLE the value of the piece."

I so wanted that vase. Self-knowledge is akin to self-loathing, for to know oneself is to know one's darker reaches, one's soiled and squalid recesses, one's feculent subconscious. Did I want the vase because it was a thing of beauty that would look *just so* on my tallboy? Or was I drawn to the piece because of Cyril, because something about him stirred my wish to belong, my desire not to be beaten down by those stronger than I, my need to be liked?

Cyril mistook my contemplative silence for a clever bargaining ploy. He put the vase back on the table. "Look", he said, "you seem like a man of the world. You've been around. You've seen things that would make me eyes go POP, I'd scarcely imagine. You and I both know this vase is worth way more than a gazelle and three score." He placed his arm around my shoulder, casting a look hither and thither, as if insuring that no other was listening. "I will let you take this away, and I'd be robbing myself, for a pair of tapirs and an otter. Done?" He spat on his palm and extended his hand.

"I have to be honest," I said. Me, *honest*? What did I know of *honesty*? My whole life was a lie. The affairs, the secret trips to Monaco, the Philippine investments that went south—my wife had lied to me about all of them. "I don't quite know what, in money terms, a pair of tapirs and an otter amounts to..."

\*

Those were my last words at the

Haverinsham Market that day. I was laughed out of the place. The fat man behind the bookstall went pink with mirth, near swallowed his toothpick. Passers-by pointed and chortled, my pain was their gain. One woman brought her child to me and lectured him that I was a lesson, what he would become if he didn't wash behind his ears and take his cod-liver oil like a good boy. Cyril...that was a different story.

A faraway look misted over Cyril's eyes, a fog of melancholy. A single tear welled up and then descended his craggy cheeks. "Go. Just go," he said, turning his head as if ashamed to see me. So I left.

When I got home I found that my wife had locked the doors and windows and sold the house. Years later I would learn that she was hiding in the cheese cupboard all along. It was a cheese cupboard in a different house forty miles away but, nevertheless, when the news reached me something inside me died. My liver, to be precise.

With nowhere to live and no living relatives—I was an orphan who was adopted by a nice couple who sadly were forced to abandon me when they found a prettier child—I looked to the State to provide me with succour. Not much was to be had there. The lady at the welfare counter shrugged and asked me if I realised that the national debt was now over seven dragons and a unicorn and that they couldn't afford to be subsidising deadbeats like me.

*

So this is why you find me here in such diminished circumstances, why you find me a supplicant, with failing eyesight, a shabby tramp blocking your way in your otherwise perfect life. But for my ignorance of an argot that marginalised me, I might have worn your comfortable brogues, your dashing white scarf and your confident moustache. But for a cruel twist of fate, I might have had your warm breakfast of oats and steak this morning; I might have slept in silk pyjamas on satin sheets; a warm and loving hand might have grazed mine in the night; I could have been you...or your husband. Or you mine. Or something.

Please, please...before you walk past me into your rosy future, you couldn't, erm, see you way clear to giving me a couple of field mice for a cup of tea and a hot meal?

# 21 INTERVIEW WITH THE AUTHOR

Below is a transcript of an interview for Dutch Arts programme *Het Echt Geweldig Literatuur Uur, Toch!*

The host, Melvyn Van Opscheppenn, claimed to have met Thaddeus Lovecraft in secret at his Gstaad mansion-hideaway and agreed to film the interview in a nearby studio. Many believed that Van Opscheppenn fabricated the interview to help fund his sex-change and turpentine addiction. Others were convinced that it represented a cry for help from either Lovecraft or Van Opscheppenn or the set director.

This may, or may not, be the only known interview with Thaddeus Lovecraft in existence, or not.

[Opening Credits roll]
Scene: As the lights come up, we see Melvyn in the distance, wearing a tweed suit and painting a fence. He stops and sniffs the brush.

[Quick Close-up: Melvyn's left eye, dilating.]
[Camera pulls back. Melvyn's head is now in shot. Soft Focus.]

Melvyn: This week, ja, in an exclusive, we shall be talking with reclusive author Thaddeus Lovecraft. Famed writer of such books as *The Unbearable Sheitness of Being*, *Rum Humour/Rum Humor and Lovecraft's Master of Humorous Prose*, he has not been seen by anyone but his chiropodist since 1995.

[Camera pans left to a setting sun.]
[Music: Copland's *Fanfare for the Common Man*]
[Montage of people holding Thaddeus Lovecraft books. Some are smiling, some are creased up with laughter. Finish with small child crying.]
Cut to interview set: Two basic leather chairs, a small table with two glasses, a jug

of water, two ashtrays and a crystal bowl filled with broccoli and an egg. One half of the set is bathed in light, the other is bathed in dark. Melvyn is sitting in the light side, nodding and talking to the person sitting on the dark side. We can make out only the contours of the person, who appears to be wearing a bobble-hat.

[Melvyn looks to camera]

Melvyn: Ja. Good evening. I am here today in beautiful Switzerland, luxurious Gstaad and I am to be speaking to Thaddeus Lovecraft, reclusive author.

[Melvyn turns to address Lovecraft]

Melvyn: Thaddeus, I'm a big, big fan. Let me tell you it is a great pleasure for me to be here talking with you today. We have a format, as all our watchers know, based on Pivot's series *"Bouillon de Culture"*. I will ask you ten questions and you will answer, shortly or, how you say, briefly. Ja?

Lovecraft: Ja...I mean *yes*. Yes.

Melvyn: What is your favourite word?

Lovecraft: Reinheitsgebot.

Melvyn: What is your least favourite word?

Lovecraft: Pus.

[SFX: Klaxon]
[Lights flash in studio. Sparkly confetti and streamers fill the air. A yellow sign circled with flashing bulbs and bearing the word *PUS* descends from the ceiling.]
[Melvyn stands, picks up an ashtray and hurls it at someone or something off-set. He swears colourfully in Dutch. He sits, throwing his comb-over back into position with a flourish.]

Melvyn: My humble apologies, ja. The show that filmed here this morning was a quiz show and the word of the day was *pus*. You must have set it off. Again, apologies. [Melvyn casts a murderous glance off-set.]

[The yellow sign bearing the word PUS withdraws upwards but creaks to a halt half-way, remaining in shot.]

Lovecraft: That's ok. I'm used to it.

Melvyn: What, can you tell me, turns you on creatively, spiritually or emotionally?

Lovecraft: Strangulation, domination, fetish-play, Richard Widmark.

Melvyn: What turns you off?

Lovecraft: Switches.

Melvyn: What is your favourite curse word?

Lovecraft: <barely audible words whispered>

Melvyn: Ja, sorry, could you repeat that?

Lovecraft: <barely audible words whispered>

Melvyn: What sound or noise do - Wait, what did you say?

Lovecraft: <barely audible words whispered>

[Melvyn stands, rubs palms on thighs, fixes bowtie, fixes cufflinks. Takes off jacket. Rolls

up sleeves, cufflinks pinging left and right.
Picks up last remaining ashtray. Shakes it at
Lovecraft. ]
Melvyn: You bastard. You complete bastard.
I didn't ask to be this way. It is just who I
am. You shit.

[Melvyn places hand on ear. Message
perhaps being relayed from off-set. He looks
at Lovecraft. He presses firmly on his
earpiece. He listens. He puts down the
ashtray and fixes his comb-over. He sits
down. A bead of sweat trails down his left
cheek.]

Melvyn: Ja. Ja. It appears you said <barely
audible words> but what I heard was
<barely audible words>. Ha ha.

Lovecraft: That's perfectly ok. Happens all
the time.

Melvyn: So...What sound or noise do you
hate?

Lovecraft: Phil Collins.

Melvyn: Right...What profession, other than

your own, would you like to attempt?

Lovecraft: Bobble-hat vendor.

Melvyn: What profession would you not like to do?

Lovecraft: Groom of the Stool. Look it up. It's a real thing.

Melvyn: If heaven exists, what would you like to hear God say when you arrive at the pearly gates?

Lovecraft: It wasn't your fault.

Melvyn: Well that's all we have time for, this week. Join us next week when we will be having the conversation with pop superstar Rick Astley. Ja!

[Melvyn turns to Lovecraft as the credits roll. We do not hear the conversation they are having but Melvyn opens the top buttons of his shirt and points his nipple at Lovecraft with menace.]

...CUT.

**This page deliberately left blank.**

**This page accidentally left blank.**

**Not sure what is going on with this page.**

**This page is taking bloody liberties.**

## Page of Lists:

Use this page to keep a record of toiletries
that you have deliberately or accidentally
consumed during the reading of this book.

_____
_____
_____
_____
_____
_____
_____
_____
_____
_____
_____
_____
_____
_____
_____
_____
_____

## ABOUT THE AUTHOR

It is believed that Thaddeus Lovecraft was born in Ireland sometime between January 1965 and October 1972. Although some researchers cling fast to the claim that he was home-schooled, there is growing support for the theory that he received no formal education whatsoever. Notwithstanding this limitation, he entered Trinity College Dublin in September 1990. Later that day he was asked to leave as they were closing up for the night.

The rest of Lovecraft's life is shrouded in mystery. It is known that his parents were killed in a freak hairdressing accident and that he has used his vast inheritance to protect himself from the outside world ever since.

Several mail-order brides were bought with his credit card in March 1997 but all were returned in their original packaging before the 28-day period had elapsed.

## ALSO AVAILABLE FROM
## PILLAR INTERNATIONAL PUBLISHING

Last Orders at the Changamire Arms
by
Robin Walker


Lovecraft's Masters of Humorous Prose
by
Thaddeus Lovecraft


The Young Dictator
by
Rhys Hughes


Books available on Amazon.com
and
In all good bookshops